GET IN
THE GAME

A Woman's Introduction to Golf and Finding Love on the Course

Dwayne Gatlin

Printed in the United States of America

First Printing, 2014

ISBN 13: 978-0692279021
ISBN 10: 0692279024

Published by: Remarkable Author Press
www.remarkableauthor.com

Remarkable Author
Transforming Ordinary People
into Extraordinary Authors

Table of Contents

Special Offer

After you've learned what characteristics you are observing and you've identified a potential partner, take our quiz to find out if he's a good match for you.

To download the quiz and get a first date recipe, go to www.golfanddating.com/thankyou

Foreword

Ladies, let me tell you that this man knows what he is talking about. I know – he's my husband. I actually met him on the golf course. At the time, I had just moved to Atlanta and was looking for a way to meet new people while learning a sport that I had always wanted to play.

I've watched Dwayne use golf as a great equalizer. Just talking about golf opens up doors for business and breaks down barriers with people who may assume that you have nothing in common. Playing golf gives you the chance to have big conversations in a relaxed setting. Most importantly, if you pay attention, you will learn who a person is just by watching them play.

Dwayne has talked about this information for a long time and he's always giving tips to his students about what to look for in a mate. He's finally put his information into a book so that others can benefit. I'm so proud of him.

I urge you to not just read the information – pay attention to what is being presented to you and be smart.

Blessings,

Jenai Gatlin

Introduction

With so many dating sites, dating apps, books, talk shows and seminars, it's no wonder so many women get discouraged after meeting a man who's nothing like his profile. Good looks, a good job and lots of money do nothing to truly reveal a man's true character. There's never a 100% fool-proof way to be certain that a man is who he says he is, but, what if there was a better way to improve these odds and put you in line to meet Mr. Right?

You've probably read articles or talked to friends that suggested that there are plenty of men playing golf. What better place to meet a man and find out who he really is at the same time? You've heard that when a man shows up for a date, what you are really seeing is his "representative". This is the person who is on their best behavior during the early stages of getting to know each other. It's just about impossible to hide one's true character on the golf course so this is a great place to assess the person you are meeting.

You may wonder at this point, "How do I get myself in the company of a man that plays golf and not be a distraction? Do I just go to the golf course and simply hang out? Do I join a golf League? What do I do to meet these men Dwayne? I'm sure that these are only a few questions on your mind and I hope that I have piqued your curiosity. Many of my students, 95% of whom are women, ask me how they can meet some of those gorgeous men they see going in and out of the club house and on the course, driving those electric carts, chasing that little white ball. You will be surprised to find that it's a very simple process, one that you will find very interesting. Well, keep reading and I'll show you how….

(Note: Because ladies are reading this book and looking at the male golfer, I will refer to a golfer in the masculine – his, he, him, etc.)

Why Does Anyone Play?

How can anyone enjoy hours chasing a little white ball around a big field trying to get it in a little hole? Well, I have to tell you that some 25 million men and women across the U.S enjoy the game of golf, a game found to be self-rewarding on so many levels. Self-fulfillment is one of the core reasons people play this sport because it challenges one's self through motivation, which at times is a difficult task. Golf is game that requires 85 % to 90% mental effort to succeed. Men and women love this game because it's comparable to life in so many ways.

Golf Measures Character

Many of you are familiar with golf only because of a few well-known names such as Tiger Woods, Jack Nicholas, and Arnold Palmer, but for the most part that's as far as it goes. Golf is a sport that reveals many virtues of a person that plays the game - integrity, patience, respect, self-control, slow to anger, to name a few. Just know, golfers cannot leave their beliefs and values behind when they head out to the course. A belief is something accepted as true without certainty of proof; a value is something important to each individual, and serves as a guide to making decisions.

Indications of Character

As mentioned from the outset, golf requires character, because it mirrors life challenges and how we deal with them.

Is He Trustworthy?

Let me share a funny story about character. I was at a card party and there were several ladies and gentlemen meeting for the first time, all having a pretty good time. About eight of us decided to play a card game called Tonk with the stakes of a penny per hand. After about an hour of playing, one guy, who was down a whopping 15-cent got caught cheating, keeping extra cards in his lap. His response was "Hell, it was only pennies!" Now ladies, what does this say about this man? Well, we all felt and let it be known to the young lady that he was pursuing that this was a red flag in regard to his character. The kicker was that about three weeks later he was fired from his job for theft - how ironic. Ladies, please don't ignore the signs.

When it comes to character and being on the golf course, the golfer playing spends most of his time alone doing activities such as preparing to hit his golf shot, looking for his ball in the woods, recording his score, or simply following the rules of golf. Most times, his playing companions aren't even paying attention to how many times he hit the ball or whether or not he moved the ball or other infringements of the rules. So if you see something that looks questionable, ask yourself, "If he cheats on the golf course, why wouldn't he cheat on simple issues regarding life?" After all, golf is an individual sport; we are simply playing against our own self and trying to beat the golf course. How can a person get satisfaction knowing full well that he recorded scores that were false or that he broke several rules during his round and then brag to others about a score that's not honest? Now, a lot of you have no clue at this point of scoring or the basic rules of the game, but hang on, I'll give you that information a little later so that you can have an edge up on the evaluation process.

Does He Show Care & Respect?

When on the golf course with your date, you will get to notice a person's temperament. Does he get mad quickly after making a mistake? Does he display childish behavior and temper tantrums by cursing, slamming down or throwing clubs? Do you notice mood swings throughout the round? Now, it's one thing to be disappointed and passionate, but moody and downright irate is another.

I remember meeting an NFL pro trainer at my golf facility. I initially thought that he was a good guy. He had recently taken up the game and visited my facility several times and we seemed to hit it off. I decided to invite him to play a round of golf with me and some friends and I was shocked at what I saw. The transformation in this guy was unbelievable. After hitting a bad shot, he started throwing clubs, cursing and became very moody. He didn't record the correct score and since a grown man knows how to count from one to ten, his lack of honesty was obvious. This was a very disappointing experience for me and my friends.

The most saddening part of this was the fact that I had prematurely introduced him to a good friend of mine, and she was scheduled to go out on a date that same night after our round of golf. Well, after *the representative* showed up for the first three dates, the real person began to show himself. My friend noticed the mood swings, the bursts of anger while driving, the disrespect towards the valet, and the lies she overheard him telling over the phone. Wow! These were some of the same characteristics I experienced with him on the golf course. Now, please don't take this as saying that all actions on the golf are an indication of how a man will ultimately treat you, but, I will say, unless he has a split personality, it will be pretty close to his real disposition and you should take some time to really explore this person's character.

Is He A Good Citizen? Is He Fair?

When golfers hit the links, the number one goal is to beat the golf course. You usually play in groups of two or four and each player tries to beat the golf course's targeted score by shooting your best score for that round, therefore, competition is born. Even though you are playing against others, you don't wish for your playing companions to hit bad shots and you don't wish for poor play for your playing partners. If you were to see your date constantly badgering others or thoroughly enjoying the mistakes of others, maybe that's something you want to observe more closely because you never know, you could be the person that makes a mistake and you are the one being pounced upon.

Is He Patient?

If you meet someone that plays golf and want to give you lessons, take him up on it. This may be a good time to see how patient he is and how well he communicates. So often I've seen and heard that the person's love interest gets irritated when the person that they are trying to teach doesn't pick up the game quickly enough. In fact, it may be that the student is not learning because the "teacher's" communication skills are not clear and precise. Remember, you want to see Patience and Understanding.

The tempo of a man's golf game is often dictated by his personality. Tempo refers to his pace of play and the energy of his being. A man's tempo will give you a clue about his level of patience. Does he display a sense of urgency? Does he pace between shots or walk extra fast? What is his general demeanor when waiting for others like his playing partners or others in front of him?

Is He Self-Disciplined? Is He Responsible?

Can you trust that your companion will do the right thing by following the rules when no one is looking? Does he do what he is supposed to do? Let's say you're on the golf course watching your person of interest, and you notice that he moves the ball with his foot or club to improve his lie before hitting his shot. Or, you see him hit the ball a total of five times to get it in the hole, but yet he puts down a score of four. First of all, he violated the rules by moving the ball before hitting it; secondly, he recorded the wrong score. Learning the basic rules of golf will allow you to evaluate whether or not he's following the most apparent rules.

Places to Meet

So, now that you know the qualities you're looking to observe, where exactly do you meet the men?

At the Course

Most men like to hang out with their buddies and play golf, however, believe me when I say that playing golf with his lady from time to time is a man's dream.

Meeting at a golf driving range is a great ice breaker, and also an opportunity to show off your knowledge of the game by asking questions and making observations about a man's swing.

Some courses offer clinics for beginners and specialty aspects of the game. I've done several golf clinics for women only and had lots of single men show up to watch and lend a helping hand. I've seen love connections made and even three resulting marriages (including my own!). These couples now enjoy playing golf together in tournaments and on vacation.

After taking some basic lessons, check with the local courses to find out if they offer mixed leagues. Playing in a mixed group of men and women not only offers you the chance to observe how a potential mate interacts with others, you can gain valuable friendships and playing partners in the other women who are playing. Plus, you are working on both your individual game and learning to play as part of a team.

If mixed leagues aren't an option, find out when men's leagues start and show up at the driving range about an hour before their start time to practice.

Another way to find a match at the course is to either call ahead and ask to be paired with someone or just show up to play. You will be classified as a walk on standby and paired with another single or put into a group of three to make a foursome.

Tournaments

Tournaments, whether hosted by companies or professional associations are a great way to meet men from your company or line of work that may not be in your everyday view.

> *Tip: Many people who play in tournaments are being sponsored by their company or are business owners themselves trying to make business connections on the course. Those that are representing their company at the tournament have often achieved a certain level of management (and we should assume financial status) that gives them the privilege of playing.*

Many charities also sponsor tournaments as a way to raise money. Look for a cause that you care about and there will often be spots available for you to play.

Tournaments are often associated with fund-raising and the tickets are often more expensive than you might normally pay for a round of golf but there are a few extra benefits. These include 1) playing on a course that you might not normally play on because of some type of exclusivity, 2) the opportunity to network during the registration and breakfast time, and 3) more mingling during the lunch and awards ceremony. After the tournament, golfers are all trickling into the luncheon area and turning in their scorecards at staggered times, depending on when they finish their last hole. This is a great time to mix and mingle and have lunch with others who were not in your golfing group.

> *Tip: If you can't afford to play in the tournament, ask if volunteers are needed. It still puts you in the same space as the people you're trying to meet. There are often no-shows on the day of the event and some tournaments may ask if any of the volunteers want to play golf so that all golfers have a partner. Have your clubs in the car at all times!*

Online

There are online sites that match golfers up for just a friendly round of golf or for romantic matches with golf as a unifying interest. Check out the following sites:

American Singles Golf Association

Dateagolfer.com

Golfingdates.com

Golfmates.com

Greatgolfdates.com

Singlegolfersclub.com

Singlegolfersclub.com

Meetup.com

Facebook

Icebreaker Questions

Do you know any good golf courses in _____?

I get invited to my company tournaments but I haven't mastered the game yet. Can you recommend a teacher?

I find this game interesting. Can I watch you hit a few balls?

I'm curious, why do you enjoy this game?

Do you have any advice on how to get started playing golf?

Do you like playing golf with ladies?

Can I play a round with you?

Learning to Play

If you know of a friend that plays the game, ask if you can hang out and watch them play. Also take a notepad and ask questions. If you don't know a friend, call or visit a golf course. When you call the course, you are calling the pro shop. Let them know that you are interested in learning the game and you'd like to have someone walk a few holes with you when the golf course isn't busy to get a feel for the course surroundings.

Make sure to ask about check in, pricing, and when and how to schedule a tee time. Pick up a score card and ask the course pro about scoring. The objective of the visit is to familiarize yourself will everything in regards to the golf course.

While there, be sure to check out the practice area. You will definitely find men practicing their game. This might be a chance to introduce yourself to someone you find attractive, even at this beginning stage. It's best to learn the game before proceeding, but hey, who can deny love at first sight?

Finding a Teacher

To learn golf quickly, it's a good idea to find a trained professional golf teacher, one that specializes in teaching beginner golfers. This golf pro will help you learn how to swing the club correctly and suggest the right equipment for you to buy. You will also need to know about the rules and etiquette of the golf game.

The cost of lessons will vary depending on the teacher credentials, the type of lessons and where the lessons take place. There are different types of lessons such as individual, small group, clinics and golf school. I always suggest staring with a beginner's clinic and then transitioning to individual lessons. After receiving the basics from the golf clinic you can now hone in on your own individual program to tailor your personal growth.

To find a teacher and get the most from your lessons there are a few pointers to follow:

1. Golf professionals will most likely work at a golf course or practice range.

2. Ask friends and acquaintances to recommend someone.

3. Before booking a lesson, contact the golf pro to find out if he or she works with new golfers. Ask for references.

4. Communicate with your instructor . about your expectations and ask how the two of you will track your progress.

5. Make sure that your teacher is compatible with you and is willing to help you achieve your expectations. They should be encouraging you and motivating you in a manner that you find positive for helping your achieve your goals. Remember, you are spending your money and you want to feel good about your purchase. If you and your instructor are not a good fit, move on.

6. Ideally the instructor includes time on the practice

range, homework to include drills, and written golf terminology. You also want at least one lesson playing a few holes on the golf course.

Golf Equipment

Equipment such as clubs, bags, balls, tees, gloves and shoes is essential if you are serious about learning the game. Having golf clubs that fit is very important because we all have different physical make ups and having the clubs fitted for you will be important for future growth.

Your golf pro should be able to suggest clubs to buy and where to buy them. If there is a pro shop on site that sells equipment, they will most likely suggest that you start there. General sporting goods stores and specialty golf shops also carry a wide selection of clubs in various price ranges.

Used sporting equipment stores such as Play It Again Sports will also have a selection of golf equipment. You can always get a used set of clubs now and have them adjusted by a club maker at a specialty golf shop or other places that make and repair clubs.

Whichever route you take, make sure that you are getting some advice from someone who is knowledgeable about equipment.

You're not shopping for the most or least expensive thing on the shelf. Before buying, be sure to ask about the return policy.

Getting a used set of clubs for now won't hinder you from getting the clubs adjusted for you from a club maker at places such as PGA Super store, Golf Smith, Edwin Watts and other places that make and repair clubs.

Golf Attire

Golf attire for women is so important because it creates a first and lasting impression. You don't want your outfits to be over the top or too revealing, but you can be sexy. A sexy woman correctly holding a club, correctly swinging a club and knowing some golf terminology will get you noticed very quickly.

In addition to specialty sports stores and pro shops, you can now find golf attire in discount stores. You would for any other outing. Be pulled together, color coordinated and have your clothes fitting well. Sexy does not mean too tight to move in – you don't want to have to adjust your clothes after each move you make.

Speaking of sexy attire, make sure you know how to move around in your clothing. You will not be bending down to place or retrieve your ball the same way a man does. You should take one small step forward with one foot and bend down at the knees, using your legs and not your waist. There's nothing wrong with a little sexy flirtation – just make sure that you are not over the top so as not to be disrespectful or risk being disrespected.

Golf Etiquette

The history of golf tradition is expressed by its rules and etiquette. These rules were created to place emphasis on civilized behavior, honesty and integrity. Bending the rules or cheating is especially strong because remember, golf is a game in which one really plays against one's self.

Here are some general rules to remember while on the golf course. You are not only taking your partner into consideration but also, others, especially behind you, on the golf course.

1. Turn off the cell phone.

2. Avoid slow play by keeping your practice swings to a minimum, hitting your ball as soon as you're ready, and keeping search time for lost balls to less than 5 minutes. If your pace of play is much slower than the rest of your group, you may need to pick up the ball and not finish the hole. Play "ready golf" (hit when ready, even if you aren't away) until you reach

the green, be prepared to play when it's your turn on the tee and green, and never search for a lost ball for more than five minutes.

3. Be mindful of other golfers taking swings. Within your group, stand still and far behind the player at the tee box. While riding in the golf cart, stop the cart if you come upon a player getting ready to swing.

4. Play to your ability and keep competition friendly. You don't have to play

down your ability but you want to be gracious if you are winning. There's a way to win without being obnoxious. (If your date can't handle you winning, this should be a warning sign for you to act like the gingerbread man. Run!

Golf Terminology

Golf terminology is important because it solidifies the fact that you know golf enough to be among real golfers, it's just that simple. Remember you are there to surround yourself around men that play the game of golf and to better position yourself to evaluate his character. Knowing the terminology and basic rules of the game will give you that edge for your evaluation. Basic terms and definitions that you should know are listed at the end of this book.

Golf as A Comparison to Life

Golf has many rewards and benefits. Beside the pure enjoyment, millions of people find the game to be rewarding because of the excitement, challenges and fun while playing alone or in the company of others. Golf is a game that is a mirror of life's challenges and how we deal with them. This game teaches us to live life simply, yet with purpose. In golf, we plan our shot, clear our minds, swing, watch the results and move on. In life, we learn to think ahead, to focus on what we're doing, evaluate what we've done, and move on to the next activity.

We must be reminded to keep things in perspective - we are there to enjoy the game, ourselves and the company of others. Anything can happen on the golf course. A shot can bounce off a tree and end up in the rough or can bounce right back into the fairway with a clear shot to the green. We're reminded that we must take the good with the bad, move on and make the best of it.

In golf as in life, we look to improve ourselves. In golf we look to improve our scores, not become angry or distracted and keep our head in the game. In our lives, we strive to have a more joyous and productive existence. This is the common thread that weaves through golf and life - development and expression of our potential.

Using Golf to Evaluate the Man

So ladies, as you put yourself in positions to meet men, playing the game of golf is certainly more enjoyable than hanging out in the bar and club scene. There's certainly a mental and physical enjoyment that you derive while being outdoors playing the sport. As you begin to get acquainted with other golfers and find playing partners, you are able to evaluate a potential future mate in a non-threatening but competitive environment where you will definitely see clues as to who he really is unfold in front of you. Is anyone perfect? No, certainly not, but if you pay attention to a man during his golf game, you can get some insight as to who he really is. What you ultimately decide that you can live with is up to you, but don't say I didn't tell you. Love and Golf go hand in hand, you just have to find it..........

Basic Golf Terms and Definitions

Address - Your position in relation to the ball as you prepare to strike.

Alignment - How your body is aligned in relation to an imagined ball-to-target line.

Approach shot - One whose target is the green.

Backspin - The spin on the ball caused by the loft of the club face.

Backswing - The first part of the swing, when the club is taken away from the ball to behind the shoulder.

Birdie - A score of one under par on a hole.

Blind - A hole or shot where you can't see your target.

Bogey - A score of one over par on a hole.

Bunker - A natural or artificial depression on a fairway or round the green. It is usually half-filled with sand but can be made of earth or grass.

Caddie - A helper who carries a player's bag around the course and may advise on the course or the game.

Chip - A lofted shot played from around the green. Usually played with a pitching wedge or a sand wedge.

Chip and run - A low shot that runs towards the flag played from near the green.

Clubface - The area of the club that you use to hit the ball.

Clubhead - The part of the club attached to the lower end of the shaft, and used for striking the ball.

Collar - Edge of a sand hazard.

Cup - The tubular lining sunk in the hole. Also the hole itself.

Deep stuff - Grass left to grow so that off-line shots are made more difficult. Also called 'rough'.

Divot - A chunk of turf removed by the clubhead when you play a shot, usually on the fairway.

Dog-leg - A hole with a fairway that bends sharply. A hazard is often positioned at the angle of the dog-leg to put you off driving across it.

Double bogey - A score of two over par for a hole.

Downswing - The part of the golf swing from the top of the backswing to striking the ball.

Draw - A shot with a slight, controlled curve through the air, from right to left for a right-handed player and right to left for a left-handed player.

Drive - A shot which is played from the tee, usually with a driver (a 1 wood).

Driver - The 1 wood, the most powerful club in the set, used for getting maximum distance off the tee.

Drop - When a ball must be lifted under penalty or otherwise, the player, standing erect, holds the ball at arm's length and shoulder height and drops it making sure that it does not land any nearer the hole.

Eagle - A score of two under par on a hole.

Face - The surface of the clubhead that strikes the ball.

Fade - A shot designed the curve slightly in the air, from left to right for a right-handed player and right to left for a left-handed player.

Fairway - The cut grass, and proper route, between the tee and green.

Fairway woods - 2, 3, 4, 5, and sometimes higher-numbered woods designed to be used when the ball is in play after the tee shot.

Flagstick - Also called the pin, flag, or stick, the flagstick marks the hole.

Follow-through - The part of the swing beyond impact with the ball.

"Fore!" - The shouted word by which golfers warn others on the course that they are in danger of being hit by the ball.

Foursome - A matchplay or strokeplay game between two sides of two players each, the partners striking the ball alternately.

Fringe - The collar of slightly longer grass around the close-mown putting surface of the green.

Full set - The 14 clubs which are allowed for playing a round. A full set usually consists of three or four wooden clubs or metal woods, nine or ten irons and a putter.

Get legs - A term shouted by a golfer when a shot just made is assumed to be short of the intended goal.

Gimmee - Baby talk for "give me," a putt of two feet or less that a friendly opponent declares does not have to be holed out.

Grain - The angle at which the grass of a green grows. Putting "against the grain" requires more effort than "with the grain."

Green - The closely mown, carefully manicured target area in which the hole is cut.

Grip - The part of the club you hold, and the way you hold it.

Handicap - A system devised to make play between golfers of different standards an even match. Your handicap is the number of strokes over par you average over four rounds at a golf course. For instance, if your average score is 88 on a par 72 course, you are given a handicap of 16.

Hazard - A bunker, stream, ditch, lake, or pond are all hazards.

Heel - The part of the clubhead beneath the end of the shaft.

Hole - This can mean the actual hole that you putt into or the entire area between tee and green.

Hole Handicap - Each score card indicates a handicap number for each hole. The lower the number, the harder the hole is to play.

Hook - Faulty stoke when the ball curves to the left for right-handed players and right for left-handed players.

Iron - Irons are metal-headed clubs used for most shots between tee and green. Sometimes you can use them from the tee at holes where accuracy is more important than distance. The sand and pitching wedges are also irons.

Lie - Where the ball is in relation to the ground it is resting on. The more embedded in the grass or sand the ball is, the worse the lie. Lie also refers to the angle of the sole of the clubhead to the shaft.

Links - A seaside golf course, typified by sand, turf, and course grass, of the kind where golf was originally played.

Loft - The angle of the clubface to the ground. The more loft a club has (indicated by how high the number is on the club) the higher the ball goes and the shorter distance it travels.

Long game - Shots over about 180 yards (164m) long, played from the tee or on the fairway with woods or low-numbered irons.

Mark - To identify the spot on the green where a player has picked up a ball for cleaning or to clear the way for another player's putt.

Matchplay - A game between two players or two sides which is determined by the number of holes won or lost.

Mulligan - A second shot permitted without penalty. Usually only one is allowed per round and is limited to tee shots although the number can be agreed upon by players before the round begins.

Out of bounds - A ball is out of bounds if it lands anywhere prohibited for play - Usually beyond the courses boundaries.

Par - The standard score for a hole, usually based on its length. Holes up to 250 yards (228m) long are par 3's, up to 475 yards (434m) par 4's and any longer than that are par 5's. Course committees are now authorized to vary par when a hole's difficulty warrants not sticking rigidly to the distances laid down.

Penalty - In strokeplay, a rule infringement usually costs two strokes; in matchplay, the hole is generally lost.

Pin - Informal name for the flagstick in the hole.

Pitch - A reasonably high shot onto the green, traveling anything from a few yards to 120 yards

Pitching wedge - A short iron with a large degree of loft, used for pitching high but short shots onto the green.

Play-off - If a competition ends with a tie, the winner is decided by playing further holes. Currently, the winner is usually the first competitor to win a hole. The U.S. and British Opens are exceptions.

Provisional - A ball played when it seems likely that the preceding shot is lost or out of bounds. It will count, plus a penalty.

Putt - The rolling shot taken on the green, with a putter.

Rating/Slope - The United States Golf Association has committees all over the country that go to member courses to evaluate and assign each course a rating and slope. The course rating is based on a course's difficulty for a scratch golfer, and the slope rating is the measure of difficulty for a non-scratch golfer. The USGA says that a course with a 113 slope rating is one of average playing difficulty. Slope ratings can range between 55 and 155.

Reading the green - Looking at the slope and contours of the green to decide the line and speed of your putt.

Rough - Grass left to grow so that off-line shots are made more difficult. Also called 'deep stuff'.

Sand trap - Alternate name for a bunker.

Sand wedge - Also called a sand iron, the shortest, most lofted iron used for playing out of bunkers and for very short pitch shots.

Scramble - Team competition in which all players play from the site of their team's best drive, best second shot, and so on.

Scratch player - A golfer with a handicap of zero.

Shaft - The length of the club down to the clubhead.

Shank - Area of an iron's clubhead at the hosel; hence a shot hit by the clubface at this point, which flies off to the right (right-handed player).

Short game - Chipping, pitching, bunker play and putting on the green and around it up to a distance of 100 yards (90m) away.

Slice - Faulty shot which curves left to right in the air (right-handed player).

Square - When the clubface is placed at right angles to the imaginary ball-to-target line.

Stance - The position of your feet just before playing a shot.

Stroke - A shot in golf.

Takeaway - The start of the backswing.

Tee - The area of a hole from which you play the first shot.

Tempo - The timing and rhythm of your swing, which should be even and smooth throughout.

Top - A shot mistakenly hit with the bottom edge of the club, so that the ball is embedded in the ground before popping up, and in most cases traveling only a short distance.

Trap - A sand bunker.

Unplayable - A player may choose to deem a ball unplayable, taking a penalty stroke and dropping the ball no nearer the hole. A ball that is unplayable in a bunker must be dropped in the bunker or stroke and distance taken.

Uphill lie - When a ball is positioned on ground sloping up ahead of the player.

Waggle - A player's loosening-up movements at address.

Wedge - A club with an extremely lofted face (pitching and sand irons).

Whiff - A complete miss of the ball on a swing. Also called a fan.

Wood - A club normally used for distance shots. It can be made of wood, metal, or graphite.

Yardage (distance) chart - A plan of the holes on a course showing the distance from one point to another. It can be printed by the course or prepared by the golfer or his caddie.

Acknowledgements

Thank you to:

Denise Haley for research

Tyrone Swain, General Manger
Brown's Mill Golf Course (American Golf)
Atlanta, GA

My wife, Jenai Gatlin

Remarkable Author Press

About The Author

Dwayne Gatlin is a professional golfer, golf instructor, observer of human nature and self-proclaimed relationship expert. Dwayne coaches and teaches beginners to advanced level players in the metro Atlanta area. Over the year, he's taught a number of women who have gravitated to the sport as a way of meeting men while his single male students openly share their struggles of meeting the right woman. As a result of listening to his students and observing character traits, Dwayne has been able to match three couples who later married. Now he shares his knowledge with you.

For more golf tips and dating advice, connect with him at:

www.dwaynegatlingolf.com
www.golfanddating.com

7267276R00046

Printed in Great Britain
by Amazon.co.uk, Ltd.,
Marston Gate.